WONDER VERSE

Freedom Of Words

Edited By Byron Tobolik

First published in Great Britain in 2025 by:

Young Writers
Remus House
Coltsfoot Drive
Peterborough
PE2 9BF
Telephone: 01733 890066
Website: www.youngwriters.co.uk

Book Design by Ashley Janson

Softback ISBN 978-1-83685-183-7
Printed and bound in the UK by BookPrintingUK
Website: www.bookprintinguk.com
YB0626F

FOREWORD

WELCOME READER,

For Young Writers' latest competition *Wonderverse*, we asked primary school pupils to explore their creativity and write a poem on any topic that inspired them. They rose to the challenge magnificently with some going even further and writing stories too! The result is this fantastic collection of writing in a variety of styles.

Here at Young Writers our aim is to encourage creativity in children and to inspire a love of the written word, so it's great to get such an amazing response, with some absolutely fantastic pieces. This open theme of this competition allowed them to write freely about something they are interested in, which we know helps to engage kids and get them writing. Within these pages you'll find a variety of topics, from hopes, fears and dreams, to favourite things and worlds of imagination. The result is a collection of brilliant writing that showcases the creativity and writing ability of the next generation.

I'd like to congratulate all the young writers in this anthology, I hope this inspires them to continue with their creative writing.

CONTENTS

Athelney Primary School, London

Nokaiah Williams (11) 1
Murjana Tajudeen Ahmed (10) 2
Rachael Oladinni (10) 4
Nyilah Guthrie-Marshall (11) 5
Aminat 6
Duc Nguyen (10) 7
Max Smyth-Barker (11) 8
Bella (10) 9
Angel (11) 10
Iryna Komarenko (11) 11
Sanjyan Yokeswaran (10) 12
Hailey Cherry (10) 13
Cody Earle 14
Mari Sidorova (11) 15
Shamar Taylor-Blades (11) 16
Zubair (10) 17
Owen (10) 18
Rachael Oladinni (10) 19

Godstone Primary & Nursery School, Godstone

Logan Connolly (7) 20
Woody Obee (7) 21
Dante Erceg (8) 22
Annabelle Marsh (7) 23
Matilda Roffey (7) 24
Amelia Snowden (7) 25
Leo Gibson (7) 26
Griffin Prince (8) 27
Elsie Flynn (7) 28
Chloe Lewis (8) 29
Evie Lancaster (7) 30
Owen Thomas (7) 31
Ella Shade (7) 32
Emily Norman (7) 33
Riley Jex (7) 34
Kiyan Patel (7) 35
Finley Budd (7) 36

Gordonstoun Prep School, Duffus

Lucy Hays (9) 37
Phoebe Shepherd (10) 38
Riya Manoj (9) 39
Florence Taylor (9) 40
Olivia Overton 41
Zara Wood (9) 42
Ron Rose 43
Amaya Murphy Leckie (10) 44
Arrawen Whyte (9) 45
Hermione Garbutt 46

Halterworth Primary School, Romsey

Tilly Cook (10) 47
Noah Robinson (9) 48
Benjamin Spratt (9) 50
Blake Lusty (8) 51
Amy Lester (9) 52
Emma Hewitt (9) 53
Esme Davison (10) 54
Frankie Stephens (9) 55
Deva Palat (9) 56
Max Houghton (9) 57
Kaeleigh-Ann Parker-Baker (9) 58
Evelyn Sanders (10) 59
George Gowman (9) 60
Henry Brunnschweiler (9) 61

Francesca Hawkes (9) 62
Lilly Meader (9) 63
Joshua Chaffey (10) 64
Ella Dance (9) 65
TJ King (9) 66
Adam Rushforth (9) 67
Imogen Tatham-Eason (9) 68
Abi Ollason (10) 69
Louie Conie (9) 70
Jenna Beckett (9) 71
Eloise Barrett (9) 72
Olivia Bryant (9) 73
Polly Adams (9) 74
Alexander Keyes (9) 75
Douglas Quayle (10) 76
Bella Cavill (9) 77
Kobi Hunter (9) 78
Lilly Blaxill (9) 79
Erin Young (9) 80
Holly Blaker (10) 81
Jessica Pitman (9) 82
Seren Vavasour (9) 83
Sami Knight (9) 84
Neave Bell (9) 85
Vivi Hunter (9) 86
Thomas Sharvill (9) 87
Hannah Mellor (10) 88
Lila Sotoudeh (9) 89
William Hayes (9) 90
Liam Sotoudeh (9) 91
Ted Morris (9) 92

Jameah Girls Academy, Leicester

Aayat Khan (9) 93
Haya Mohamed Razvi (9) 94
Yusra Muhammad (10) 96

Kenmore Park Junior School, Kenton

Marina Bonte (9) 97
Nikhil Kabawala (9) 98
Rana Omied (9) 99
Shahad Fahad Rashid (9) 100
Rebeca Rusu (10) 101

Kesh Primary School, Kesh

Darcey Maguire (8) 102
Erica Lunny (8) 103
Maisy Moynihan (9) 104
Katie O'Connor (9) 105
Rhys Irvine (8) 106
Ellie Thompson (8) 107
Carla Simpson (8) 108
Jemma Longworth (9) 110
Archie Dickson (8) 111
Georgie Stevenson (9) 112
Jack Simpson (9) 113
Patrick Pedroso (9) 114
Faye Murphy (8) 115
Ben Gibson (8) 116
Harry Weir (9) 117
Isaac Knox (9) 118
Brooke Timlin (8) 119
Timmy Vaitkevicius (8) 120
Emily Jennings (9) 121
Johnny Walmsley (9) 122
Cody Noble (8) 123
Arthur Law (8) 124
Morgan Lucas (8) 125
Amy Likely (9) 126
Barney Phillips (8) 127
Lucas Kerr (8) 128

Linnvale Primary School, Clydebank

Krystal Young (9) 129
Bethany Downie (11) 130
Hollie Neill (11) 131
Ella Tees (10) 132
Leah McColgan (10) 133

Macmerry Primary School, Macmerry

Caitlyn Tweedie (11) 134
Brodie Dryburgh (11) 135
Halle Liddle (10) 136
Brodie Cross (11) 137
Aaron Hardie (10) 138
Josh Taylor (11) 139

Manor Oak Primary School, St Mary Cray

Brandon Laczko (10) 140
Ethan Hoad (9) 141
Hannah Nwadazie (9) 142
Ryan Maharjan (9) 143

Meadow Park School, Whitley

Grace Glennon (11) 144

Mile Cross Primary School, Norwich

Layla Cornwell (11) 145

Southam St James CE Primary School, Southam

Lucy McGurk (7) 146
Millie Macdonald (7) 147
Matthew Chorlton (7) 148
Tammy Washbrook (8) 149
Ava-May Howchin (7) 150
Jackson Walklett (8) 151
Skyla Smith (7) 152
Amelia Watson (7) 153
Dexter Gale (7) 154
Henry Woodward (7) 155
Grace Burns (7) 156
Thomas Wilson (8) 157
Albie Murphy Parker (7) 158
James Whittaker (7) 159
Jonah Phipps (7) 160
Hettie Henshaw (7) 161
Alana Harvey-Badger (7) 162

St Francis Of Assisi Catholic Primary School, Crawley

Debbie Wong (9) 163

St John Bosco Arts College, Croxteth

Klara Laniewska (12) 165

Talbot House Children's Charity, Walbottle

Jenson (9) 166
Matthew (7) 167
Johnny (8) 168
Skiilah (10) 169
Charlie (8) 170
Harry (11) 171
Nemi (11) 172
Hayden (11) 173
Summa (10) 174
James L (9) 175
Joey (10) 176
Kaden (8) 177
James J (10) 178

Tynecastle High School, Edinburgh

Hend Zaid (12) 179

Ursuline Preparatory School, Warley

Anaisha Kaul Rathi (8) 180
Maxim Bowler (9) 182
Oliver Browne (8) 184
Mia Holme (8) 186
Katerina Stowe-Mici (8) 187
Matilda Owolabi (7) 188
Nolah Mann (8) 189

Ranveer Sandhu (8) 190
Henry Chase (7) 191
Iyla Dhillon (7) 192
Theadora Peers (8) 193

VLC, Leamington Spa

Ryley Owen (11) 194

Yarlside Academy, Barrow-In-Furness

Rosie Benn (8) 195

THE CREATIVE WRITING

Child Of The Arosa Star

Under the warmth of the hot Caribbean sun,
Child of the Arosa Star,
Ripe, delicious coconut trees calling my name.

In the night sky, above the cloud,
Child of the Arosa Star,
Birds waving 'hi'.

Under the trees are blossoms,
Child of the Arosa Star,
Flowers seeking love.

Think of story time
And coconut water.

Breeze rushing through the trees,
And you splish-splashing
In the water.

Eating black-eyed peas stew
With rice and callaloo.

Child of the Arosa Star,
What will happen if
I open the door to the future?

Nokaiah Williams (11)
Athelney Primary School, London

Windrush Child

Behind you,
Windrush child,
The island of Jamaica waving goodbye.

Around you,
Windrush child,
Family of yours and family of mine.

Above you,
Windrush child,
The birds asking you why.

Hot afternoons enjoying fresh mango,
Grandma is always with you,
Not outside playing bingo.

What if they give you an unwelcome stare?
The cruelty, you cannot bear.
What if the mother country does not want you there?
What if they don't care?

Behind you,
Windrush child,
The island of Jamaica waving goodbye.

Around you,
Windrush child,
Family of yours and family of mine.

Above you,
Windrush child,
The birds asking you why.

From under the moon,
And over the sea,
You'll always have a place in my heart,
Grandma and mango tree.

Murjana Tajudeen Ahmed (10)
Athelney Primary School, London

Child Of The Arosa Star

Over the sea,
Under the sea,
Child of the Arosa Star.

If you fall in the deep, dark sea,
You can always count on me,
Child of the Arosa Star.

The mangoes fall in despair,
While the birds gasp for air,
Child of the Arosa Star.

The doors open ready for the future,
Cannot wait to see you in beautiful England.

The warm England,
Grandma always said you need.

Child of the Arosa Star,
Remember the past, get ready for the future.

Rachael Oladinni (10)
Athelney Primary School, London

What Is It?

Is it as big as an elephant?
Is it as wet as a shark?
Is it as heavy as a mountain?
Is it all bite but no bark?
Can it swim?
Can it not?
Is it as strong as a well-tied knot?
Maybe,
Just maybe,
It's exactly what I think.
If I'm very strong,
I can fit it in my sink.
I think I know!
I think I do!
I'm guessing it's a hippopotamus,
From all of the clues.

Nyilah Guthrie-Marshall (11)
Athelney Primary School, London

The Mysterious Hat

Oh mysterious hat, what do you contain?
Oh mysterious hat, what can I gain?
Oh mysterious hat, why so plain?
Mysterious hat, are you good or bad?
Mysterious hat, when I look, will I be happy or sad?
Will it be the best treasure known to man,
Or will it be worthless like a grain of sand?
I have opened you up,
And I have seen what you are.
And are you a bat?
No, you are a mysterious hat!

Aminat
Athelney Primary School, London

The Scary Village

I was in a scary village,
I found a chest,
Inside it was a sword and a bow,
To shoot at a monster.

I found a portal,
That led me inside.
A gigantic dragon -
I had to fight the boss.

I used the sword,
But it was no use.
I used TNT,
To blow up the tower.

It was destroyed,
The dragon died,
I made it!

Duc Nguyen (10)
Athelney Primary School, London

I Am Possible

I ncredible, I am

A mazing, I am
M agnificent, I am

P ositive, I am
O ptimistic, I am
S ensible, I am
S upportive, I am
I ncredible, I am
B elievable, I am
L ikeable, I am
E xcellent, I am.

Max Smyth-Barker (11)
Athelney Primary School, London

The Dragon House

The mysterious, scaly protector,
Take a candle and warm the cave,
Shining its light upon the cave,
You can see the light in the cave,
The predator flies around its cave,
It is a friendly dragon,
Looking for its owner,
It shines a candle,
So its master can find it.

Bella (10)
Athelney Primary School, London

Messi

For me and a lot of people,
Messi is the best.
But I recognise that,
For some people,
Cristiano Ronaldo
Is the best,
And I accept that
Because that's their opinion
And I respect that.
I won't tell people,
Who they have to support.

Angel (11)
Athelney Primary School, London

The Sunny Day

Somewhere on the field,
Under the bright sun,
On the fresh green grass,
Children are playing, cheering, shouting.
Somewhere on this sunny day,
With a beautiful blue sky,
Clouds are flying in the air,
Trees are waving goodbye,
For one last time.

Iryna Komarenko (11)
Athelney Primary School, London

Samurai

S amurai are sly and cunning
A fter their mission, they train
M aster said they don't feel pain
U sually, they train, then they eat
R un as fast as a lion
A ssassins come, but die
I am your nightmare.

Sanjyan Yokeswaran (10)
Athelney Primary School, London

January Times

J anuary is a frosty time
A time when I shine
N ew years begin
U nbelievable weather appears
A s new days go
R ed fingers show; remember, it's past December
Y es, this is January, my January.

Hailey Cherry (10)
Athelney Primary School, London

Football

He's fast,
He's a good finisher,
Corner kick taker,
Maybe a Ballon d'Or winner,
White-haired baller,
Good skills,
Scares people when versus people,
And plays for the Red Devils,
Meet Alejandro Garnacho.

Cody Earle
Athelney Primary School, London

Autumn

A beautiful season
U nique season that brings me cheer
T ime for leaves to sway and fall
U nbelievable beauty for us all
M iraculous times once a year
N ever hate to bring us cheer!

Mari Sidorova (11)
Athelney Primary School, London

My School

M iraculous
Y ou know we're the best

S uper
C ool
H ilarious
O h, very peculiar
O bviously amazing
L ies if someone says we're a bad community.

Shamar Taylor-Blades (11)
Athelney Primary School, London

My Animal Riddle

The creature has a long blue body.
The creature smells like the ocean.
The creature has sharp teeth.
The creature may eat people.
The creature's name starts with an S.
It is a shark!

Zubair (10)
Athelney Primary School, London

Henry Danger

One time, I was looking for an after school job,
My boss was the best superhero in town,
And I was his sidekick!
This was the first mission I got,
Super and never lost!

Owen (10)
Athelney Primary School, London

Love

L ook at me
O nly one I see
V ery, very extraordinary
E veryone should be like you.

Rachael Oladinni (10)
Athelney Primary School, London

The Basilisk

B lack like a thousand nights
A nimal made for killing
S uper slitherer
I t's a big bad beast
L ikely to kill you
I t's made to attack
S lithering through the trees
K illing machine.

Logan Connolly (7)
Godstone Primary & Nursery School, Godstone

The Basilisk

B ig, spooky, bold skin
A nimal that is frightening
S *sss!* went the basilisk
I mportant creature
L egendary reptile
I nteresting hiss
S caly skin
K illing machine.

Woody Obee (7)
Godstone Primary & Nursery School, Godstone

The Cyclops

C harismatic to people
Y ou can be scared
C aveman killer
L ying around the pillar
O n the dirty ground
P owerful hands and evil head
S winging his club around his cave.

Dante Erceg (8)
Godstone Primary & Nursery School, Godstone

The Pegasus

P owerful wings
E asily flying high
G iant feather
A s strong as a dragon
S ize of a mountain
U nusual
S ounds like a roar.

Annabelle Marsh (7)
Godstone Primary & Nursery School, Godstone

The Phoenix

P oisonous bird
H appy but dangerous
O nly one around
E xtremely deadly
N ight vision
I ncredibly scary
e **X** pert flyer.

Matilda Roffey (7)
Godstone Primary & Nursery School, Godstone

Pegasus

P leasant creature
E legant wings
G lows in the dark
A n expert flyer
S oars through the clouds
U nicorn-like
S illy.

Amelia Snowden (7)
Godstone Primary & Nursery School, Godstone

Phoenix

P owerful wings
H igh-flying
O ver the clouds
E xtra feathers
N ight eyes
I ncredible claws
e X traordinary body.

Leo Gibson (7)
Godstone Primary & Nursery School, Godstone

The Phoenix

P owerful wings
H ot fire
O range fur
E xpert killer
N ight hunter
I ncredibly dangerous
e **X** tremely deadly.

Griffin Prince (8)
Godstone Primary & Nursery School, Godstone

The Pegasus

P owerful
E legant and mighty
G reat flying
A naughty girl
S o red
U ses lots of fire
S eriously fluffy.

Elsie Flynn (7)
Godstone Primary & Nursery School, Godstone

The Phoenix

P owerful flyer
H ot wings
O range fire
E legant thing
N ice flyer
I ncredible wings
e **X** cellent bird.

Chloe Lewis (8)
Godstone Primary & Nursery School, Godstone

The Cyclops

C reepy
Y ou would be scared
C reepy
L azy
O rganised
P ointy horns
S cary.

Evie Lancaster (7)
Godstone Primary & Nursery School, Godstone

The Cyclops

A kennings poem

Caveman killer,
Evil creature,
Bone smasher,
Head basher,
Furious fighter,
Angry annoyer,
Mythical master.

Owen Thomas (7)
Godstone Primary & Nursery School, Godstone

The Phoenix

A kennings poem

Cool ashes,
Monstrous fire,
Flame thrower,
Cloud glider,
Wind crusher,
Fierce creature,
Flaming beast.

Ella Shade (7)
Godstone Primary & Nursery School, Godstone

The Basilisk

A kennings poem

Wild creature,
Frightening snake,
Piercing eyes,
Destructive monster,
Malicious beast,
Legendary animal.

Emily Norman (7)
Godstone Primary & Nursery School, Godstone

The Cyclops

A kennings poem

Fat thing,
Bat swinger,
One eye,
Dangerous thing,
Head crusher,
Fierce monster,
Ugly beast.

Riley Jex (7)
Godstone Primary & Nursery School, Godstone

The Cyclops

A kennings poem

Furiously scary,
Evil and dangerous,
Big giant,
Mythical creature,
Weird animal,
Chunky tummy.

Kiyan Patel (7)
Godstone Primary & Nursery School, Godstone

The Phoenix

A kennings poem

Frightening beast,
Flaming glider,
Destructive flyer,
Beady eyes,
Magical flame.

Finley Budd (7)
Godstone Primary & Nursery School, Godstone

I Am Poem

I am the eyes dripping with anger,
Waiting to observe death.

I am the mouth tasting blood,
With one word, you're *dead*.

I am the nose, bloody slits
Smelling hatred as I go past.

I am the pale skin, poisoned and green,
Ready to scratch you with my talons.

I am the mind, devilish and dark,
Waiting to plan murder.

I am the eyes, dripping with anger,
Waiting to observe death.

Lucy Hays (9)
Gordonstoun Prep School, Duffus

I Am Poem

I am the eyes watching the endless night,
Seeing the owls flying ahead in the mirk.

I am the mouth, dark and cold,
Sucking up light and blowing out shadow.

I am the nose finding the good,
Smelling the bad of the universe.

I am the pale skin, young and cold,
Waiting for devastation to strike the stars.

I am the mind, fiery and jealous,
Witty as a comet and as stubborn as a moon.

Phoebe Shepherd (10)
Gordonstoun Prep School, Duffus

I Am Poem

I am the eyes smeared with hatred,
Glaring with tormented impatience.

I am the mouth hissed with savagery,
Threatened with bloody wrath.

I am the nose drifted to violence,
Smelling irritated blood-filled souls.

I am pale skin, mysterious and terrifying,
Crushed throughout the rusted land.

I am the mind, plotted with jealousy,
Crushing those with torture.

Riya Manoj (9)
Gordonstoun Prep School, Duffus

I Am Poem

I am the dark, unruly mind,
Hunting down the terrible, restless light.

I am the eyes, burning like black,
Embers in the fire.

I am the tongue,
Licking an open wound with dark, sticking blood
pulsing inside.

I am the legs,
Slinking sneakily to the unexpected and unwanted
battle ahead.

I am the soul,
Hunting through the deathly darkness, seeking
revenge.

Florence Taylor (9)
Gordonstoun Prep School, Duffus

I Am Poem

I am the eyes glowing with anger,
Seeing the fright come up from toe to scar.

I am the mouth tasting the fiery red blood,
As she falls asleep forever.

I am the nose, snake slits
Smelling the regret.

I am the dark skin taking all the happy spirit,
Putting them in a dark void.

I am the mastermind, the thought of death is fun,
Plotting my devious plan.

Olivia Overton
Gordonstoun Prep School, Duffus

I Am Poem

I am the eyes glaring with jealousy,
Waiting for my moment to strike.

I am the mouth oozing with great hatred,
Tasting a broken heart.

I am the nose smelling pure anger,
In the breeze blowing towards me.

I am the pale soft skin,
Feeling sick with dark red blood on my hands.

I am the evil mind, obsessively thinking,
Plotting my ever so kind revenge.

Zara Wood (9)
Gordonstoun Prep School, Duffus

I Am Poem

I am the eyes filled with glistening sparkles,
On the paint of the fiery red Lamborghini.

I am the frail nose,
Smelling the rotten flesh of the dead people.

I am the pale cut hand,
Holding a glistening, red, blood-covered knife.

I am the mouth,
Oozing with radioactive residue.

I am the mind, mischievous and jealous,
Thinking of the joy of driving a night-black Koenigsegg.

Ron Rose
Gordonstoun Prep School, Duffus

Dementor

I am the eyes, filled with hatred,
Staring sharply at people.

I am the legs,
Drifting through flamboyant fire.

I am the nose,
Smelling evil and jealousy.

I am the arms,
Shoving and pushing frightened people into the deep, dark seas.

I am the mouth,
Sucking happiness away from the world.

Amaya Murphy Leckie (10)
Gordonstoun Prep School, Duffus

I Am Poem

I am the eyes, scarlet dark,
Dingy with anger.

I am the mouth, dark red,
Gloomy and as cold as ice.

I am the nose, blood red like blood pouring,
Smelling the blood and fear.

I am the pale skin, weak and dark,
Overcome with venom.

I am the mind, dark as the night sky,
Evil and irritating.

Arrawen Whyte (9)
Gordonstoun Prep School, Duffus

I Am Poem

I am the eyes, filled with flaming
Red fire, staring at blood.

I am the teeth, dripping blood drops
As my tongue catches it.

I am the nose, smelling dead people
As blood squeezes from their bodies.

I am the mind controlling innocent people
As they fall into the sharp, spiky rocks.

Hermione Garbutt
Gordonstoun Prep School, Duffus

A Stargazer's View

I see a planet,
I see a star,
I look up to a world,
That I know goes afar.

Underneath a time-worn sun,
A comet makes its way,
A shimmering trail of fairy dust,
Igniting night and day.

I look to the north,
From Ursa Major,
A greeting of a guide,
Who has served many in wager.

This guru is known globally,
From top to bottom,
Named the North Star,
And will never be forgotten.

Past the sight of our gravity beyond,
Past the planets to what we respond,
Past the unknown life of Mars,
Lies secrets as many as notes we play on our guitars.

Tilly Cook (10)
Halterworth Primary School, Romsey

Mo The Cleaning Robot

Many, many years ago,
A spaceship blasted off this realm,
To find a better one.
Many years, they stayed in space.
They kept flying, flying, flying,
But alas, the pod kept on going.
They flew and flew and flew and flew,
To the point where robots were invented.
NASA said, "Send Mo, he will keep them contented.
He will clean the ship, dust the walls,
And protect them from the massive balls.
Pilot the ship, maybe form a relationship."
They sent him up; he began the trial,
But the astronauts were very vile.
He started cleaning,
But Mo saw a yellow smile gleaming.
The cosmonaut kicked poor Mo,
But then, he started to have a fit.
Mo didn't find this funny.
That night, Mo pushed him out of the cosmopod.
"Quick, someone help me!"
But Mo decided to leave him be.

To this day, he is whizzing on a comet,
Whining his little head off.

Noah Robinson (9)
Halterworth Primary School, Romsey

Space

S pace goes on and on forever
P eople love space but you have to learn all the rules
A lways wear spacesuits; otherwise, you may die
C reate new things to live in space if you want
E xploring space is very dangerous.

Amazing wondrous space,
Shiny wondrous shooting stars,
The fierce flames on the wondrous shiny shooting stars,
Floating shiny diamonds,
Like diamonds in the sky,
He bubbled from inside the star,
Like a shooting star,
Like Uranus,
Does Earth have eyes lurking inside?

Benjamin Spratt (9)
Halterworth Primary School, Romsey

The Space Match

They landed on the moon for the best football match in history. The moon was the best football stadium for 4.53 light years. Every alien was watching.
As the game kicked off, number 20 was on the ball. He dribbled past his opponents and scored a superb goal. Then, a random guy called Jeff landed on the moon, got the ball in the face, and then fell off.
When the other team got a penalty, would they make the game a draw? As soon as he kicked it, an asteroid landed on his foot. It was so powerful, it went through his foot and destroyed the moon. Everyone died.

Blake Lusty (8)
Halterworth Primary School, Romsey

Space's Secrets

Look at our glistening, gleaming moon,
From Earth, it looks like you can put it on a silver sparkling spoon,

The aliens are coming from their planet,
Maybe their moons are made from granite,

The astronauts are up in space,
They see the aliens and pull a face,

The aliens try to hide away,
Because they don't want to give away,

That they are another species,
Because they have done graffiti,

Whilst back on Earth, we sit and ponder,
What's space like? I wonder.

Amy Lester (9)
Halterworth Primary School, Romsey

Silliness In Space!

Look, loads of stars!
It also includes Mars.
The moon is made of cheese!
Hang on, don't tease.

Astronauts hanging upside down like bats,
trying to tuck in their plaits!
We're inside the Milky Way,
trying to get away!

Look, a UFO!
Wait, is that a rhino?
Rockets flying everywhere!
Is there any room in there?

Aliens poking their heads out of the moon,
I'm wondering if they're having a good afternoon!
Darkness inside the universe,
it looks like a curse!

Emma Hewitt (9)
Halterworth Primary School, Romsey

Animals Of Life

A ntelopes gallop as swiftly as light, leaving the hissing as they didn't want a fright
N ewts as slippery as soap, at the top of the pond is where they float
I guanas' eyes are as dark as night, be careful as they may bite!
M onkey manoeuvre from vine to vine, moving as fast as time
A lligators swim through the night, the might in their jaw will leave you in awe
L eopards leap onto a tree, excited for their treat - a chunk of meat
S nakes slither in through the soft sand.

Esme Davison (10)
Halterworth Primary School, Romsey

Space Myths

Space is known for its moon,
But is the moon really made out of cheese?
Mmm, that sounds yummy,
But I will pass.

Puzzled thoughts come into my head,
When I think about aliens;
If they're real,
I would really like an alien friend.

Astraeus is the god of space;
I really want to be the god of space,
Because I'm really good at space facts.

The centre of our solar system is the sun,
But is the sun really yellow?
No, it's actually white.
I know, crazy.

Frankie Stephens (9)
Halterworth Primary School, Romsey

Oh, Nature

N ature; as beautiful as the moon
A ll love, all care, all dirty
T hough they save, they never care
U nbearable we sometimes are, sheltering babies and moms
R ain helps us too, but not all the time; climate change is drying the rivers out
E nd of our life; millions of forests getting chopped; lots of animals losing their homes.

We give you oxygen, and this is what we get;
If this continues, there'll be no nature or humans alive,
So please take care of us.

Deva Palat (9)
Halterworth Primary School, Romsey

Aliens And An Astronaut

The astronaut landed on the moon,
And started walking along the surface.
Then he turns and sees,
Something that looks like peas.
He follows them home;
They are bigger than gnomes,
He goes inside their homes and sees bones.
An alien dog appears through the fog.
He grabs the bones and runs to the gnomes.
They stand still with no bills.
The astronaut has fun and runs to the pool,
It's cool but he has to leave,
So he heaves a rock.

Max Houghton (9)
Halterworth Primary School, Romsey

Space Dream

A young girl went to bed and then she slept,
Dreams, oh dreams, they never come true.
Dreams, oh dreams, they are building you.
That young girl dreamt of space,
She had happiness all over her face.
Space is magic, space is great,
The moon or the sun or anything else.
The girl woke up and danced around,
And then she appreciated the sun and moon,
So that's how she dreamed, that's how she learned,
That it's here to guide you.

Kaeleigh-Ann Parker-Baker (9)
Halterworth Primary School, Romsey

The Forest

Inside the forest's undergrowth,
It's a most wonderful place,
With bushes and burrows,
Yet not a single human trace,
But through the middle,
Is a magical lake,
At the bottom is a marvellous spindle.
One day, there was a horrid earthquake,
The trees fell from the sky,
It was a horrid sight,
All the creatures gave out a cry,
Yet they fought with all their might,
And they saved the forest.

Evelyn Sanders (10)
Halterworth Primary School, Romsey

Rainforest

R owdy rainforests
A re all over the world
I n rainforests, there are lots of
N eon-coloured fish in the water but
F lying above the canopy are blue-bellied toucans,
but finally,
O n the ground, there are snakes and tigers,
sometimes you can see
R acoons in the rainforest on the
E dge of the rainforest
S lowly, the wind blew
T o rustle the leaves.

George Gowman (9)
Halterworth Primary School, Romsey

Moon Football

The referee's whistle tooted like a train, *whoop!*
The goalkeeper flew around the goal in a loop.
When the clouds below looked gloomy,
The player did a Spinaroonie.
Number eight jumped into space,
Just enough time to tie his shoelace.
Bosh, as a player scored a goal,
An alien popped up to see, just like a mole.
Penalty for number nine to try,
While an asteroid whistled by.

Henry Brunnschweiler (9)
Halterworth Primary School, Romsey

Space

In space, you can see so much,
I can see so many stars,
I can see so many planets,
I can see the whole solar system.
I can see a black hole,
Look at excellent Earth from up here,
I can see so much from up in space.
Look at the craters on the moon,
Look at all the amazing asteroids.
Wow, I can see all the stars in the whole of space.
Look at the moon and the comets,
It looks amazing.

Francesca Hawkes (9)
Halterworth Primary School, Romsey

The Beautiful Kingfisher

The colourful, rainbow kingfisher zoomed past the colourful canopy of greens.
Its vibrant body attracts every single animal in the rainforest,
But all the animals try to keep up with the kingfisher.
The colourful canopy swarmed with birds at night,
The colourful canopy swayed in the wind at night,
The colourful canopy was surrounded by lianas,
But the kingfisher was still a butterfly after so many years.

Lilly Meader (9)
Halterworth Primary School, Romsey

Kittens' Playtime

Little fluffballs roll about;
Ending up in a massive mount.

Fluffy bundles of playfulness,
Cute and cuddly, curious.

Quiet and friendly, silent and stealthy;
Running through the night, legendary.

Your door is locked but cats are your key,
'Cause they bring smiles to you and me.

Different shapes and sizes;
Equals lots of varieties.

Joshua Chaffey (10)
Halterworth Primary School, Romsey

The Galaxy

Did you know that space is a magical place?
The twinkly stars, magnificent moon and the pretty planets are even more breathtaking than you think.
The sun may look like a big, bright ball in the sky, but it's actually a large star.
There are so many interesting facts about space that a fair amount of us don't know about.
I wonder what scientists will find out in the future.

Ella Dance (9)
Halterworth Primary School, Romsey

Decomposers

D ead things, they decompose
E verything meets them eventually
C hemicals are what they use
O nly certain species do this job
M any are fungi
P eople fear them for they mean death
O nly some have brains
S lowly, they work in silence
E verything they work with
R eturns to the ground eventually.

TJ King (9)
Halterworth Primary School, Romsey

Hydrothermal Vents!

Deep below,
Vast oceans,
Biomes lay,
Boiling biomes,
Brilliant biomes,
Breathtaking biomes,
Hydrothermal vents!
Claustrophobic caves,
Of crystal spikes,
Packed with:
Bursting bubbles,
Like volcanoes,
Crazily causing,
Crabs flying,
Eelpouts flying,
Alvinella pompejana flying,
Prodigious!

Adam Rushforth (9)
Halterworth Primary School, Romsey

Crybaby's House

Quietness creeps through Crybaby's house,
Except for Crybaby's bedroom.
The TV is static, her house is dramatic,
But she didn't realise her mum wasn't home.
Crybaby cries in sync with the vines,
Growing through the top of her walls.
Sooner or later, her house is overgrowing,
And Crybaby is stuck forever.

Imogen Tatham-Eason (9)
Halterworth Primary School, Romsey

Ocelot!

The fierce black teeth were knives,
Hunts glorious rabbits, rodents and fish,
Rests in the cool canopy in the day,
And is crepuscular at night when it hunts,
Its silky spotted coat blends into the bush,
This ocelot is territorial, so watch out,
Take care of this creative creature,
Because we lose them all the time.

Abi Ollason (10)
Halterworth Primary School, Romsey

Space

I n space, the stars are shiny
N ow, on Earth, the time is timely

S ucking stuff, black holes do
P icking up the pace, light does
A cing it all, astronauts do
C limate changing, Earth does
E ffortlessly orbiting, the solar system does.

That is *space.*

Louie Conie (9)
Halterworth Primary School, Romsey

The Woods

Me, my sister and my mother live in a cottage in the middle of nowhere inside the forest.
One night, my sister and I decided to go into the woods and play hide-and-seek. So we wandered into the woods and the first round was fun, but I realised that she was taking me further into the woods.
All of a sudden, *poof!* She was gone...

Jenna Beckett (9)
Halterworth Primary School, Romsey

Rainforest Tiger

T errifically silent and
I ncredibly intelligent; I think of my moves as I
G racefully leap from branch to branch whilst I track
my prey, which allows me to
E legantly pounce and overpower my prey
R oyally delicious dinner - can you guess what I am?

Answer: A majestic tiger.

Eloise Barrett (9)
Halterworth Primary School, Romsey

Space Is Special

S uper awesome meteors, everything in space is good
P owerful rays of light, everything in space is good
A stronauts bobbing around, everything in space is good
C ool like a lightning bolt, everything in space is good
E verything in space is good.

Olivia Bryant (9)
Halterworth Primary School, Romsey

Nature

N ature has trees and leaves
A utumn is my favourite season
T he leaves turn red and yellow
U nder the ground, little bugs live
R esting animals
E normous trees burrow.

They are like green skyscrapers,
The grass was as green as the branches.

Polly Adams (9)
Halterworth Primary School, Romsey

The Mystery Collision

At hypersonic speeds, I collided,
My remains are floating through space,
The rest of me slowly dying away.

Scientists querying my existence,
Parts of me bleeding away,
Bits still buried deep somewhere in the Milky Way.

Where am I?
Who am I?

Alexander Keyes (9)
Halterworth Primary School, Romsey

The Leopards

A kennings poem

Huge crunch,
Leopard lunch,
Gorilla killer,
Climbing thriller,
Rapid runner,
Long jumper,
Very well dyed,
They walk with pride,
Large eyes,
Good disguise,
Ambush predator,
Food competitor,
Nocturnal creatures,
Pack leaders.

Douglas Quayle (10)
Halterworth Primary School, Romsey

The Green Anaconda

Inside the rowdy rainforest,
As long as a roadway,
The slippery, slimy skin moves along the ground,
It can be seen from the sky because of its eyes,
Ready to attack,
Venom hissed out of the anaconda's mouth,
High chance of living when in a fight.

Bella Cavill (9)
Halterworth Primary School, Romsey

What Am I?

I am a majestic creature,
I play in a beautiful blue lagoon,
I sleep so smoothly,
I eat snippy-snappy crayfish,
But that's not all,
I am the cutest animal
In the whole entire universe.
What am I?

Answer: I am an otter!

Kobi Hunter (9)
Halterworth Primary School, Romsey

Planets In Space

There are nine planets,
That orbit the sun -
But the people and animals,
Live on one.

Earth is our planet,
Great and old -
New and old beginnings.

And there's a star called the sun,
That keeps all the planets warm.

Lilly Blaxill (9)
Halterworth Primary School, Romsey

Space

S uper solar system where it all begins
P eaceful planets in the Milky Way circling a black hole
A mazing astronauts in the space station floating around
C urious craters made by asteroids
E legant Earth, a planet of life.

Erin Young (9)
Halterworth Primary School, Romsey

Holly Tree

T remendously
R eaching
E legantly
E njoying
S pring

S urrounding
P owerful
A rches
R ound
K ind
L ove
E xtends
D elightfully.

Holly Blaker (10)
Halterworth Primary School, Romsey

Rainforest Lizard

L ovely lizard glimmering in the moonlight
I zzy Lizzie crawling up trees
Z ooming and flying around
A ngry Lizzie flying down
R apidly in the stars, Lizzie is shining
D otty scales in the woods.

Jessica Pitman (9)
Halterworth Primary School, Romsey

Space

S ky is filled with twinkling stars
P articles are floating in the sky
A steroids bash into each other, forming debris
everywhere!
C omets whizzing past the Earth
E clipses happen once in a while.

Seren Vavasour (9)
Halterworth Primary School, Romsey

Starlight

Starlight illuminates the sky with brightness,
Like a cinema of colour,
A gargantuan space of dreams and wishes,
Like a light in a dark room,
As bright as the sun as they shine in the sky,
Filling up the sky with hope.

Sami Knight (9)
Halterworth Primary School, Romsey

Space

S pace is amazing and fun
P lanets are crazy and we live on one
A liens are odd; they have six eyes
C ool spaceship, Neil Armstrong flies
E verything is possible, so do not give up if you fail.

Neave Bell (9)
Halterworth Primary School, Romsey

The Monitor Lizard

Some called it a snake,
But it was not a snake,
It was a monitor lizard,
Appearing from the Earth,
Dug out of the drain,
A lizard,
A monitor lizard,
Robust claws and nails,
And its long, long tail.

Vivi Hunter (9)
Halterworth Primary School, Romsey

Leopard

A kennings poem

Huge crunch,
Leopard lunch,
Gorilla killer,
Climbing thriller,
Rapid runner,
Long jumper,
Camouflaged hider,
Tree rider,
Ambush predator,
Food competitor,
Powerful jaws,
Sharp claws.

Thomas Sharvill (9)
Halterworth Primary School, Romsey

My Planet In Space

A kennings poem

Earth heater,
Sky lighter,
Shadow creator,
Slow turner,
Night guard,
Ice melter,
Day increaser,
Planet puller,
Life giver,
Red Giant future.

Hannah Mellor (10)
Halterworth Primary School, Romsey

Nature

As the creature stands,
Nature surrounds.
A predator lurking in the bush,
Could this be his competitor?
He stands strong,
With his paws ready to attack!

Lila Sotoudeh (9)
Halterworth Primary School, Romsey

The Amazing Life Of Space

Space is better than any human trace,
A black hole can wipe out the human race.
Mother Nature gives us Earth,
But space gives us birth.

William Hayes (9)
Halterworth Primary School, Romsey

Stop Littering!

As many people litter,
The bins are not getting fed,
Animals are dying,
We can stop littering,
It's never too late.

Liam Sotoudeh (9)
Halterworth Primary School, Romsey

Yum, Yum!

Roses are red,
Violets are blue,
Belgian bun in my tum,
Yum, yum.

Ted Morris (9)
Halterworth Primary School, Romsey

Rainbow The Unicorn

Rainbow, its name,
She likes tie-dye,
Rainbow, its colour,
Favourite one too.

Rainbow, her name,
Galaxy, her friend,
Cotton candy, her sister,
Shadow, her brother.

Rainbow, its name,
Its beautiful colour,
Tie-dye rainbow,
Going through perfectly.

Rainbow, its name,
Rainbow, its name!

Aayat Khan (9)
Jameah Girls Academy, Leicester

The Rainbow

Red:
Ruby red, shiny like an apple
And as bright as a strawberry.

Orange:
Fiery orange sky, bright as a tangerine
And as vibrant as a flower.

Yellow:
Amazing yellow, beautiful like a daffodil
And as bright as the sun.

Green:
Emerald green, bright like a gemstone
And glossy like glass.

Blue:
Sapphire blue, bright like the clear sky
And as beautiful as a glacier.

Purple:
Galaxy purple, dark as our Milky Way
And beautiful like the ocean.

Pink:
Blush pink, beautiful like a rose
And as elegant as a dress.

Allah has created the red, orange, yellow, green,
blue, purple, and pink colours in the rainbow
for my eyes to gaze upon.
O what a beautiful sight.

All praise be to Allah
The greatest creator!

Haya Mohamed Razvi (9)
Jameah Girls Academy, Leicester

Wonderful Weathers

Winter makes it snow,
And all the plants won't grow.
In spring, plants start growing,
No more snowing.
In autumn, leaves start to fall,
So I have to start wearing my shawl.
In summer, the sun shines in the sky,
And the bees buzz high.

Yusra Muhammad (10)
Jameah Girls Academy, Leicester

Don't Be Sad, Pluto

Pluto, Pluto
Don't be upset that you're a dwarf planet,
You will make more friends.

Pluto, Pluto
Trust me,
Trust me,
Your BFF is still next to you.

Guess what? You can make friends,
Like Ceres, Makemake, Haumea, Eris,
We all know you have been
A dwarf planet since 2006 AD.

What if you have life in the future?
What if you explode before the sun?
Would you have people on you that look like ghosts?
What if you have aliens on you?
Just so you know, if you don't know about the sun,
Well, you will when the sun explodes.

Marina Bonte (9)
Kenmore Park Junior School, Kenton

My Seasons

Cold snow falls to the ground,
While snowmen are being built,
Epic snowball fights are being played,
Between you and me.

Hot chocolate is being made,
With warm cuddles,
Christmas lights are being put on,
While the weather gets colder.

Blossoms are appearing,
I blow dandelions,
They fly into the distance,
With all the others.

Animals have woken up from their hibernation,
While new animals are being born,
Huge Easter eggs are being found,
Spring is just a colourful season.

Nikhil Kabawala (9)
Kenmore Park Junior School, Kenton

The Beautiful World Of The Lunar Landings

The heavenly moon, how bright it glimmers,
That it almost shivers.
The moon has moonquakes, so it quivers,
The moon comes in all colours,
It has no brother, also no mother,
It sleeps with the stars in the sky,
That's why they only come in the night,
All of these things are so bright,
Sometimes it gives people a fright,
Now it's time to say goodnight.

Rana Omied (9)
Kenmore Park Junior School, Kenton

Amazing Me

Hello, my name is Shahad and I am in 5SA.
I am going to write about myself.
My most favourite subjects:
I think my faves are art and literacy.
But when it comes to maths,
I feel like I am going to throw up.
The place I would like to go
Is somewhere adventurous.
My life: I am a 9-year-old girl
Who loves her friends and horses.

Shahad Fahad Rashid (9)
Kenmore Park Junior School, Kenton

Rebeca's Jam

This is me
I'm unique
Yes, that's me
I ain't weak

This is me
My name's Rebeca
Yes, that's me
I'm mighty clever

This is me
I love to speak
Yes, that's me
I'm full of cheek

This is me
You know who I am
Yes, that's me
You've got my jam.

Rebeca Rusu (10)
Kenmore Park Junior School, Kenton

I Love My Pet Dog

I love my pet dog, Milo, he's like a cheetah.
In the morning when he sees us, he's so happy
And then is just fine when he's seen all of us.
He looks like chocolate that's been melted and stirred,
With little white bits like snow, it's so cute!
At night, he is as tired as a baby in his bed
And he spreads his arms and legs out with one leg up.
He is so cheeky sometimes and smells like:
A daisy, sweets, and then sometimes wet.
He is soft, cosy, fluffy, fun and weird,
And when he sees a cat, he barks like crazy
And it's funny most of the time.
He comes up to my bed at night,
And won't get off 'til my dad comes to get him down.
When I close my door, he will sit outside it
And will not go away.
He loves his ball
And plays with it until he goes to sleep.
He will get a bit of food and take it to the living room,
Then go back and get more food.
He loves his walks so much and pulls on his lead a lot,
But I still love him.
I love my pet dog, Milo, so much!

Darcey Maguire (8)
Kesh Primary School, Kesh

My Cat

I love our cat,
It comes home at lunch for food.

When the lights are turned off, I can see the light in his eyes,
It shines like a light in a village at night-time.

Our cat has spiky fur, as sharp as a knife,
He smells like grass that's just been cut.

When it is on the sofa, it lies on its back and you can see white fur,
It is as white as fresh milk out of the fridge.

When I have my fluffy blanket,
He always comes up to lie on it.

His meow is as soft as a mouse in someone's house,
Trying to find something to eat.

Sometimes it comes up to my room,
He always drools on my bed though!

He enjoys eating his treats,
He munches like a cow, happily eating watery grass.

But the best thing I love about him,
Is when he cuddles me like a teddy bear.

Erica Lunny (8)
Kesh Primary School, Kesh

My Doggy Blanket

I love my doggy blanket,
It is like fluffy pink ice cream.

It is really, really, really cosy,
I cuddle it up in my face.

The dogs have blue and brown eyes,
I just love it.

It smells of Mummy's best washing powder,
It makes me feel cosy, relaxed and calm.

It has so many dogs on it,
It matches with my bed.

The dogs look like Paddy, Aunty Gemma's dog,
I love my little doggy blanket.

It is so similar to a fluffy dog,
It is pink and really snug.

It is really special to me,
I would never give it away.

Maisy Moynihan (9)
Kesh Primary School, Kesh

I Love My Dog

He's as cute as a baby sleeping in its mother's arms,
I feel safe when I'm beside him,
He is so small and as soft as a soft blanket,
He is as white as a cloud,
I love my dog.

I love him so much because I've had him for a long time,
He smells like popcorn,
He's so happy every time I'm next to him,
He is a peach and white toy poodle,
I love my dog.

His name is Bingo,
He's so lazy and loves his food,
He loves to sit beside Mum, Dad, Amy and me,
He likes to sleep and look out of the window,
I love my dog.

Katie O'Connor (9)
Kesh Primary School, Kesh

Leeds Football Club

My favourite team is Leeds,
I think they are the best,
Sometimes they score goals against the rest.

Their usual kit is white like a fluffy cloud,
When they come on the pitch, I feel very proud.

I like them because they are the best team, go boys!
I've liked them for a long time, my dad likes them too.

The stadium is Elland Road,
It is huge like a herd of elephants.

One of their kits is orange and black like fire and coal,
The players run like Flash after the ball.

I love Leeds United!
The best team in football!

Rhys Irvine (8)
Kesh Primary School, Kesh

My Dog: Sandie

I love my dog,
Every morning, my dog and I watch TV together.

Every day when I come home from school,
She runs to me like a cheetah.

When she comes back from the groomer's,
She smells as sweet as marshmallows.

When she plays fetch with me,
She protects the ball like a mummy bear and her cub.

When the sun shines on her,
She feels as soft as snow.

She is gold like honey,
And as golden as the sunshine.

Every night, she cuddles up with me, like a teddy bear.
I love my dog.

Ellie Thompson (8)
Kesh Primary School, Kesh

I Love My Granny's Dog, Wilma

I love Wilma,
She is as soft as wool.

I love Wilma,
She is funny and fun.

I love Wilma,
She is really fast and energetic.

I love Wilma,
She smells as nice as a flower.

I love Wilma,
Her fur is brown and she's crazy like me.

I love Wilma,
She loves me back.

I love Wilma,
She is so cute.

I love Wilma,
She is just herself.

I love Wilma,
She is so cuddly and soft.

I love Wilma,
She cuddles me a lot.

Carla Simpson (8)
Kesh Primary School, Kesh

I Love My Cat

My cat is black and white like a chessboard,
She smells like roses and buttercups,
My cat is comfortable, cosy and loved.

My cat is soft like a cloud in the sky,
She loves to lie on her warm bed,
My cat lies on top of me like a fluffy blanket.

My cat begs to come in for lunch,
She brings me joy and happiness,
My cat curls up into a ball and sleeps by the fire.

My cat is squishy like a marshmallow,
She is a fluffy ball when curled up,
My cat has a deep scratch and eats like a lion.

Jemma Longworth (9)
Kesh Primary School, Kesh

My Dog: Ella

I love my dog, she smells like fresh grass.
At night, I hear her bark like she is singing.
She is fluffy and cute and likes to play.
She is orange like sand dust
And white like the white clouds.
She feels fluffy and has baby hair.
I love my dog like I love my mum and dad.
When I go to sleep,
She always goes to sleep with me.
She likes to play with a tennis ball.
She likes to go on walks to Castle Archdale.
When she eats her food,
I can hear her crunch it up.

Archie Dickson (8)
Kesh Primary School, Kesh

Louie The Pup

My favourite dog is called Louie,
Louie is very good at tricks and smells like dog food.

Louie is so fluffy, like a stuffed animal,
He lays on the carpet waiting for me to rub his belly.

He is brown like wood, black like coal and as white as milk,
He is a fast wee thing.

He is as cute as a guinea pig,
Louie will race with me up the hall and he always wins.

Louie messes with everything because he is a pup!
My favourite dog is called Louie.

Georgie Stevenson (9)
Kesh Primary School, Kesh

I Love Farming

I like farming because I like doing it with my Granda,
I like feeding the calves,
I like going on the dark green John Deere with my Granda,
I like grappling the stinky silage and feeding the calves' meal,
I like scraping the cow poo in the big shed,
I like going on the quad with a helmet on,
I like tossing the tyres off the silo pit,
I like going on the big green harvester with my dad,
I like picking blackberries on the farm,
I like going on the big red tractor.

Jack Simpson (9)
Kesh Primary School, Kesh

My Teddy From Sonic

I love my Sonic teddy.
Every day, I always play with it,
Even when I get back from school.
It is yellow like the shining sun,
And smells like pancakes.
I always hug it when I watch TV,
And when I go to bed.
It has a big smile,
Like children playing with their friends.
When I had a playdate with Lucas,
We played with my teddies.
I love my teddy because I got it for my birthday
And it is my favourite toy.
I love my Sonic teddy.

Patrick Pedroso (9)
Kesh Primary School, Kesh

I Love My Toy Bunny

I love my toy bunny, it is as white as a cloud in the sky,
My toy bunny is as soft as fluff,
I love to cuddle it when I put it on my face at night.

My toy bunny makes me feel safe at night,
I love my toy bunny because it used to be my mum's
and now it is mine,
When I get scared, my toy bunny makes me feel safe.

My toy bunny always makes me happy,
My toy bunny is not too big or not too small,
And that's perfect.

Faye Murphy (8)
Kesh Primary School, Kesh

I Love Man United

I love Man United because,
They have Rashford, Garnacho and Fernandes.

Their away kit is as dark as a blue whale,
And their home kit is as red as hot lava.

They're good at scoring goals with their front three,
Rashford, Garnacho and Antony.

They win a lot of trophies,
Like the FA Cup.

Their defence is good,
With Shaw, De Ligt and Martinez.

Ben Gibson (8)
Kesh Primary School, Kesh

I Love My Dog

He is as fluffy as a teddy bear,
His whiskers are as sharp as a knife,
He is a King Charles the Third.
Me, Mummy, Daddy and my dog,
Watch a movie every Friday night,
He comes over to me for popcorn.
His coat is dark brown,
He is as sneaky as a mouse,
He is as loud as a dinosaur,
He always kisses me goodnight,
He plays like a child,
He smells like the outdoors.

Harry Weir (9)
Kesh Primary School, Kesh

I Love My Pet Dog

I love my pet dog, Ruby,
Her hair is as black as coal,
Her fur shines like silver because of the lights,
She is polite and can do lots of tricks,
When we let her outside,
She always comes in with a stick,
And when she comes in, she's like a cheetah,
When we take her on walks,
She gets as dirty as a pig in mud!
I love my pet dog, Ruby.

Isaac Knox (9)
Kesh Primary School, Kesh

My Bed

I love my bed,
I sleep in it every night,
It is as warm as a fire,
It is as purple as grapes,
When it's clean,
It smells as fresh as flowers,
It is as soft as a marshmallow,
It is as fluffy as a cloud,
It is as cosy as a stick in a fire,
My bed is fluffy, cosy and purple,
When I lie in it,
I feel like a sausage in the oven.

Brooke Timlin (8)
Kesh Primary School, Kesh

I Love My Celistite

My celestite is as shiny as a star in the night sky,
As blue as the sky above,
It feels like cold metal and glass,
It's as beautiful as a rainbow,
Made of rain and sun,
Mined in Madagascar, deep underground,
Where it is as dark as coal,
It's not cut, it's raw,
On top of a stone connected to it.

Timmy Vaitkevicius (8)
Kesh Primary School, Kesh

I Love My Rabbit

I love my rabbit,
It smells like a rose in the freshest field,
At night, we cuddle up in my bed,
My rabbit is as soft as a cloud,
It is as small as a newborn baby,
It is sweeter than any other rabbit,
It is as cute as a chick and has long ears,
My rabbit looks like a fluffy cotton ball.

Emily Jennings (9)
Kesh Primary School, Kesh

My 150 Case Tractor

I love my 150 Case tractor,
I love the roar when my foot hits the floor,
It's as mucky as a pig in mud,
The tyres are as big as a mountain,
It's as fast as a leopard,
My tractor is hard-working all year round,
Sometimes, it gets bogged,
And that is no fun at all.

Johnny Walmsley (9)
Kesh Primary School, Kesh

Man United

I love Man United,
Their kit smells as fresh as their pitch.
All you can hear are the fans shouting when they win a trophy.
They have a bright red kit.
I like Man United because they have Garnacho and Onana.
They are one of the best teams in the world.
I love Man United.

Cody Noble (8)
Kesh Primary School, Kesh

I Love My Dog, Daisy

I love to play fetch with my dog in the garden,
She loves to lie on me on the sofa in the living room,
She loves to go for a walk with me at Necarne,
She likes to bark a lot and chew my bed,
She smells like grass from the field,
She is brown like dirt and white like a cloud.

Arthur Law (8)
Kesh Primary School, Kesh

My Bear

I love my bear,
It was my first bear when I was a baby.

It is yellow and it looks like gold in the sun,
It sometimes smells like grass.

It feels so fluffy and it's so cute,
It is my favourite bear.

I play outside with it,
I love my bear.

Morgan Lucas (8)
Kesh Primary School, Kesh

I Love My Teddy

My teddy is called Winnie,
He has yellow skin and a red jumper,
He is as soft as a pillow,
And as cuddly as a water bottle,
When I feel him, I feel safe,
He has black eyes like the sky at night,
And a round nose like a pancake.

Amy Likely (9)
Kesh Primary School, Kesh

I Love Burgers

I love burgers because when I bite into them,
They are so good!
I love it when I smell them, they smell so good!
They are like flowers in a field,
We usually get them in June,
I love them when they are on the barbecue.

Barney Phillips (8)
Kesh Primary School, Kesh

The Abominable Snow Menace

It is made by Beano,
It is black, red, white and blue,
It is like The Battle For Bash Street School,
It is a rectangle,
It is about a yeti,
I love it so much because I like to read.

Lucas Kerr (8)
Kesh Primary School, Kesh

My Emotions Are What Get Me By

Sometimes I'm happy,
Sometimes I'm sad,
Feeling emotional,
It isn't that bad!

When I'm happy, I laugh,
When I'm sad, I cry.
But my emotions...
They're what get me by!

I also get anxious,
I also get angry.
When I feel these emotions,
I try to breathe calmly.

Never let them build up,
Always let them show.
Express them when you feel them,
Keeping them in isn't healthy, you know!

Krystal Young (9)
Linnvale Primary School, Clydebank

I Have Friends

I have friends.
My friends are intelligent,
My friends like a cappuccino,
My friends tell the best stories,
My friends are supportive.

I have friends.
My friends will make up after an argument,
My friends will help others,
My friends are creative,
My friends know each other well.

I have friends.
My friends know me well,
My friends and I are a team,
My friends are always there for me,
My friends are the best.

Bethany Downie (11)
Linnvale Primary School, Clydebank

The Beautiful Mountains

In the mist, you will see a mountain,
The top is like a chocolate fountain.
The biggest mountain stands out bold,
But the weather there is very cold!

The trees are covered in snow,
They stand out with their eerie glow.
If you look in a cave, you will say woah!
Caves are full of wonders you will never know...

And if you look up high,
(I definitely cannot lie!)
The clearness in the sky,
It's nice to see with my eye.

Hollie Neill (11)
Linnvale Primary School, Clydebank

The Emotions Of Me

Happy one minute.
Next up?
Sad.
Excited then worried.
After that?
Anger followed by anxiety.
Then disgust.
Followed finally by embarrassment.

I will stand with my emotions,
I will understand each of these,
I need emotions in my life,
I will take these emotions by the hand,
I will use these to guide me through the world.

Ella Tees (10)
Linnvale Primary School, Clydebank

Trees Are Alive

Trees are alive,
You can hear the branches vibrating,
All the time they swish in the sky,
Loving the shining moon that looks like it's about to burst,
Year after year, they are so precious,
They have a wonderful way of life,
Giving graceful movements in the sun.

Leah McColgan (10)
Linnvale Primary School, Clydebank

My Blossom Tree

A haiku

Oh, my blossom tree,
Your pink leaves are so pretty,
You are so unique.

Caitlyn Tweedie (11)
Macmerry Primary School, Macmerry

Japan

A haiku

Mount Fuji is big,
Japanese shoes are so cool,
Noodles are so nice.

Brodie Dryburgh (11)
Macmerry Primary School, Macmerry

Japan

A haiku

Japanese noodles,
Cherry blossom all over,
Japan has earthquakes.

Halle Liddle (10)
Macmerry Primary School, Macmerry

Japan

A haiku

Welcome to Japan,
All the red and blue onis,
For the Setsubun.

Brodie Cross (11)
Macmerry Primary School, Macmerry

Japan

A haiku

Make Daruma dolls,
The teru terus do work,
Mount Fuji is cool.

Aaron Hardie (10)
Macmerry Primary School, Macmerry

Manga Art

A haiku

Welcome to Japan,
Manga originates here,
Ponyo is manga.

Josh Taylor (11)
Macmerry Primary School, Macmerry

Formula One

F1 with the fastest cars on Earth,
Zooming across the elegant tracks,
With the time just over one min.

Pressure building up by the seconds of time,
The G-force pushing on the neck,
Can Lando Norris win the rest?

Lewis Hamilton, champion of all,
Is he going to claim it overall?
Max Verstappen fighting to stay on top.

Teams having millions to start with,
Can they stay within the cost cap?
Pulling off the best strategy,
Was a tragedy at the end.

Last lap, can George Russell take the win?
And he does it with the trophy in his hands.

So now all I wonder, who is going to be the
next Champion in 2025?

Brandon Laczko (10)
Manor Oak Primary School, St Mary Cray

Wonders

W ondrous creatures in most people's dreams, some scary, some not
O n the moon, so many aliens form a plan but very secretly
N ot that we know, wondrous dragons sneak onto our precious Earth
D angerous creatures take a magical roller coaster to Earth
E aten creatures from space barely make it out alive
R eally wretched creatures that haunt us with every single dream, even good ones
S ome good, some bad; this is bad. It's the end of the poem.

Ethan Hoad (9)
Manor Oak Primary School, St Mary Cray

The Wish Puppy

There is a white wish puppy,
With bright blue eyes that glow in the dark.
When you blow on your wish, your dream comes true.
The puppy hears you and you can't believe your tears.
You will dream of touching the sky.
Up in the clouds above you,
Wishing on the stars twinkling very far.
You will be happy if you have a wish puppy.

Hannah Nwadazie (9)
Manor Oak Primary School, St Mary Cray

The Potato Poem

P otato
O verfilled
T he mashed potato
A thing you can make into fries
T his tasty vegetable
O bviously scrumptious.

Ryan Maharjan (9)
Manor Oak Primary School, St Mary Cray

Spooky Season Is Here

Spooky season is here.
The leaves turn gold,
Rain starts to fall,
Children go home in the fog
And scream whilst they play,
Some catch colds and bundle up inside.

Halloween is here.
The pumpkins start to glow,
Spiders weave their webs,
Candy is in bowls for the children
Dressed in masks and costumes,
Some stay inside in the warmth,
So, that is that.

Spooky season is here!

Grace Glennon (11)
Meadow Park School, Whitley

Trauma

"Your trauma makes you stronger!"
So I get told, but my trauma stole my childhood,
My happiness, my safety and my voice.
I was a child!
I needed to be happy and safe,
I was a child!
I didn't need to be stronger,
I needed love, support and shelter from the world.
I was a child, I couldn't change what was going on,
But I still blame myself to this day.
You hurt me and I'll never forgive you for that.
The worst part is, I hate you, but I miss you.
I was a child.

Layla Cornwell (11)
Mile Cross Primary School, Norwich

Unicorns

U nder the blanket of darkness, barely making a
N oise, unicorns gallop in gardens and
I n enchanted forests. With
C olourful horns and magical powers
O ver the fields, they glide
R unning over village roofs, playing with children
N oses of unicorns smell very good food smells
S oft unicorns have swishy tails.

Lucy McGurk (7)
Southam St James CE Primary School, Southam

The Dancer Who Lost Her Dance

The dancer
Loses her costume.
The dancer thinks she's
No good. The silly
Dancer practises
And practises
But she doesn't get better.

She's
Just started
Her dance. She
Does one dance move,
One by one. She goes to
The dance studio
Every Friday.

Millie Macdonald (7)
Southam St James CE Primary School, Southam

What Is It?

It has wings.
It can fly.
It can breathe fire.
It eats meat.
It's not a bird.
It has a tail.
It's not a dog.
It has four legs.
It has no arms.
What is it?

Answer: It is a dragon.

Matthew Chorlton (7)
Southam St James CE Primary School, Southam

What Am I?

I have water dripping out of my mouth.
I like to eat food.
I like to have a walk.
I sleep in a bed on the floor.
I wee and poo outside.
I like playing with my toys.
What am I?

Answer: I am a dog.

Tammy Washbrook (8)
Southam St James CE Primary School, Southam

Dragonfly

D ances on the wind
R ainbow of colours
A ngel wings
G entle giant
O ver the water
N ight sleeper
F ast flyer
L eaf balancer
Y esterday's hopper.

Ava-May Howchin (7)
Southam St James CE Primary School, Southam

What Am I?

I'm as tall as a skyscraper with a fiery crown,
My blazing sword could slice up a town.
With a cube-like body, I'm a very good shield,
As soon as you see me, you'll not want a fight and yield!
What am I?

Jackson Walklett (8)
Southam St James CE Primary School, Southam

Autumn

Autumn leaves turn orange and gold,
And the leaves fall off the trees,
I crunch through fallen leaves,
The smell of bonfires,
In the distance, the smoke curls up into the sky,
Conkers fall from their spiky shells.

Skyla Smith (7)
Southam St James CE Primary School, Southam

My Lion

My lion looks like a stripy cat,
My lion sounds like a tiger,
My lion feels like a soft teddy bear,
My lion tastes like a cat,
My lion smells like a fish,
My lion feels so nice.

Amelia Watson (7)
Southam St James CE Primary School, Southam

What Am I?

Terrifying monster,
Eyes burning,
Long tail,
Colossal wings,
Fire breather,
Green scales,
What am I?

Answer: I am a dragon.

Dexter Gale (7)
Southam St James CE Primary School, Southam

Seasons

A diamanté poem

Winter
Frosty, icy
Sledging, shivering, freezing
Snowballs, cold, holiday, beach
Boiling, swimming, playing
Hot, sunny
Summer.

Henry Woodward (7)
Southam St James CE Primary School, Southam

Nature

A diamanté poem

Trees
Green, brown
Flowing, rustling, waving
Tall trunks, small petals
Growing, rooting, sprouting
Bright, colourful
Flowers.

Grace Burns (7)
Southam St James CE Primary School, Southam

My Favourite Sports

A diamanté poem

Rugby
Rough, fun
Tackling, scrummaging, running
Try, team, ball, goal
Kicking, dribbling, shooting
Loud, energetic
Football.

Thomas Wilson (8)
Southam St James CE Primary School, Southam

Villages And Cities

A diamanté poem

Village
Small, quiet
Playing, boiling, baking
Houses, camping, sport, roads
Beeping, taking, buying
Big, noisy,
City.

Albie Murphy Parker (7)
Southam St James CE Primary School, Southam

Autumn

Leaves go gold and orange,
I crunch through fallen leaves,
The smell of bonfires,
In the distance, smoke curls in the sky.

James Whittaker (7)
Southam St James CE Primary School, Southam

Penguins

Penguins are furry like fabric,
Penguins have thick coats,
Penguins live in the cold,
Penguins go swimming for fish.

Jonah Phipps (7)
Southam St James CE Primary School, Southam

Elephant

Long
Swinging trunk
And bigger than
A mountain, flappy ears,
Giant footsteps, never forgets,
An elephant.

Hettie Henshaw (7)
Southam St James CE Primary School, Southam

Rain

A kennings poem

Puddle maker,
Plant grower,
Gardener's friend,
People soaker,
River filler,
Fun maker.

Alana Harvey-Badger (7)
Southam St James CE Primary School, Southam

Seasons

S wimming into spring, heat trickled onto the Earth,
which was as soothing as music
E xploring deeper and deeper into the lush meadows
A pril was rising, magnificent in the breezy air
S uddenly, unexpectedly
O ceans of flower cups were blossoming into alluring
plants
N ature was wrapping its arms around my home.

S oaring into spring, warmth illuminated the Earth
P erennials occurred against the lavish fields
R obins tweeted out into the morning
I nspiration hid at every corner
N o clouds slumbered in the skies
G rowing buds bloomed pleasantly.

S ailing into summer, the world was lively
U tilising the warmth to keep their energy alive
M aking their way through summer, a breeze
M y Earth was filled with sunshine
E veryone contributed to the buzz of comforting
chatter
R eally-loved summer whizzed by yet again.

A crisp pile of golden red leaves scattered across the forest ground
U nreliable trees whispered secrets to each other
T hey wrecked people's courage and let thousands of leaves fall
U ntil the skies were grey
M y soul was tranquil
N ot a single bright leaf rested on the trees.

W intertime approached as autumn crawled away
I dling in the cosy homes
N o one was not warming themselves near the fireplace
'T was midnight, and not a soul was awake
E lves crept in and did their job
R eceiving packages of presents, wrapping paper littered the Christmas morning.

Every season is special in its own way,
They are equally marked.
Whether it is summer, winter, autumn, or spring,
They all have a meaningful impact on the year.
Each unique season is about,
Cherishing the hidden message
And keeping it forever in your heart.

Debbie Wong (9)
St Francis Of Assisi Catholic Primary School, Crawley

Into A New World

I end the day in my bed,
Then close my eyes and dream,
A magic forest filled with trees,
And magical, furry beasts.

I walk across the bridge,
Into a little magic house,
And as I open the door,
I awaken wanting more.

I get dressed and go out to play,
Thinking about the ending along the way,
Reality can be the same,
But sometimes the stories are plain.

As a dream is like social media,
It may not always be true,
But just like social media,
It can give you the same joy too.

Klara Laniewska (12)
St John Bosco Arts College, Croxteth

Sonic The Hedgehog

S uper
O verjoyed for people who play the games
N ever had a bad game
I conic
C ool

T errific
H ow good is he?
E xcellent

H ero
E pic
D esire
G reat
E veryone loves him
H ow does he do that?
O nly one mistake in the movie
G iving happiness.

Jenson (9)
Talbot House Children's Charity, Walbottle

Heroes

T he
R obots
A re
N ot
S miley
F antastic
O utrageous
R apid
M etallic
E specially
R eally smart like a dolphin.

Matthew (7)
Talbot House Children's Charity, Walbottle

I Lost My Sanity

S ometimes you lose your sanity
A nd sometimes your sanity comes back
N o!
I lost my sanity
T he sanity never comes back for me.
Y ou just lost your sanity...

Johnny (8)
Talbot House Children's Charity, Walbottle

Home Time

H appy to be home
O pportunity to be home
M arvellous
E nd of the day

T errific
I nside
M agical
E xcited.

Skiilah (10)
Talbot House Children's Charity, Walbottle

Fortnite

F un
O ne
R un
T itle
N ice
I went for a walk
T ournament
E xciting.

Charlie (8)
Talbot House Children's Charity, Walbottle

Fave Food

C runchy
H appy
I ncredible taste
P otatoes are fresh
S oft sausages and beans are tasty with chips.

Harry (11)
Talbot House Children's Charity, Walbottle

Fab Food

C hicken
U nder our roof, I eat with Mum and Dad
R eally
R eally
Y ummy curry like blueberry cake.

Nemi (11)
Talbot House Children's Charity, Walbottle

Bouncy Kirby

K ing
I ncredible
R olls like a ball
B ouncy Kirby
Y ellow and bright.

Hayden (11)
Talbot House Children's Charity, Walbottle

My Name Is Summa, I Love Death

D angerous
E arly
A larming
T errifying
H orrible.

Summa (10)
Talbot House Children's Charity, Walbottle

Death

D angerous
E erie
A larming
T errifying
H ideous.

James L (9)
Talbot House Children's Charity, Walbottle

Death

D ie
E nemy
A ccident
T error
H orrifying.

Joey (10)
Talbot House Children's Charity, Walbottle

My Dog

D aft
O ld like a human
G reedy
S leepy.

Kaden (8)
Talbot House Children's Charity, Walbottle

Wonderful Animal

C olourful like a rainbow
O pposite to
W hite.

James J (10)
Talbot House Children's Charity, Walbottle

A Beautiful Star

A star given a sole purpose it cannot attain,
the purpose to radiate.
A star with the purpose to extend high,
with its blinding rays,
it reaches high for the bare minimum,
but cannot achieve.
A star that will not shine, what kind of star is that?
Certainly not bright enough for the humans
of our cruel society to appreciate such an outstanding star.
Such a miserable star, when will its dull stares end?
A star that cannot be beautiful,
Tell us, what makes a star?
Its qualities or its flaws?
A creation made absolutely perfect.
Tell us, how could you, who cannot shine themselves,
determine an unworthy star?
One matter of fact these beings agreed heartlessly about,
Is that when it is truly dead,
shall it be uniquely beautiful for the first time?
A beautiful end.
If only this was about stars.

Hend Zaid (12)
Tynecastle High School, Edinburgh

The Trouble With Time Travel

Have you ever heard of the day of time travel?
Where the days are bad and the nights are worse!
Like horrible history.
I *have!*
I'll tell you the story, but some bits have no glory...

I was looking out of a window when the sun was shining like gold,
And then something happened, something quite bold.
The sun turned into moon and then I touched my window gently.
Bam! It exploded with ice!
Then I got sucked in.
Boom, I looked to the side.
It was a dark and mysterious room,
My head was still hurting from when I went *boom!*

I saw a painting of a man.
Underneath it, it said Ronald Stan,
Born in 1524 and - *still alive?!*
This meant one thing, I had travelled back in time!
I saw a wardrobe without any clothes,
But instead, a key, small and gold,
Easy to lose, hard to find.
"You use it," said a voice, "I don't mind."

"I've gone back in time," I said,
"More than one hundred years!"
I've had nightmares, nightmares that are turning into fears.
I took the key and carefully put it into the hole.
Then it turned shining yellow.
I took it out quickly, but then I saw a painting
Of someone quite familiar, it was my mum!
Then I took a very close look and bent my head low,
It said, "Time travelled here - 19 years ago."
I walked around the corner and found a button.
Click - it took a picture of me.
Wow, I'm on the wall!
Then I saw this strange-looking my size door; open wide.
I pushed it and went inside.
Ooo, look at the floor, look at the room,
Ooo, look at the broken window... yahoo!
This is my house, my room, my life - woo!

Let all your thoughts about time travel
Slowly unravel...
There are many mysteries in history,
Let them evolve and *dissolve.*

Anaisha Kaul Rathi (8)
Ursuline Preparatory School, Warley

Aliens Attack Earth

Earth is safe and sound,
With people dancing on the ground.
Dancing and singing more and more,
And when people are tired, they love to snore.
On the other side are big, green, gooey monsters who are mean,
And almost look like a green bean!
They are called aliens and want to invade a planet,
And their leader was Janet.
Who was evil and cruel -
And aliens wanted to rule.
Aliens wanted to invade Earth,
So people would know their actual worth,
And sit on Earth and rule the world.
But it was curved, so the aliens would have to think more,
And that's when Janet came in and then vanished,
And nobody knows where she went.
They couldn't find her at all,
So they looked in a hall and even tried to call.
The aliens got scared,
And they were dared to go to Earth.
They had to invade and they could only find a spade.

It was going to be hard,
So they wrote Janet a card.
But soon, they found her and were lucky.
They invaded Earth, but the people got to them first.
And then they burst and got locked up in jail
And met a snail
Who was useless.
Humans had a good life
But the aliens were about to get killed with a knife!

Maxim Bowler (9)
Ursuline Preparatory School, Warley

Alien Attack

The aliens were bored, so they decided to attack Earth.
The people were having fun,
One was hairy, one was glairy,
One was snory, one was boring.
They shot laser beams - in everyone's dreams.
The aliens packed their bags because they were mad,
Because it wasn't worth attacking Earth!
Just then, the Earth returned.
Then the leaders went back to back -
One was called Zak, one was called Glack.
It was very close - for Earth to be toast.
But on the other side,
People were digging a hole, who tried
To attack but turned back after a while.
It turned into a loop -
"Turn back! Attack! Come back!"
They got sucked into Rainbow Land.
They saw planets chill,
Who chilled even when seeing Bill.
They beeped and bleeped,
And when they got back from their other attack,
The alien fell into a spiral.

But so it appeared, a man with a beard
Was left on the alien planet.
He liked to be heard and control the bird.
The people's leader fell in too,
They were stalled and appalled.
They sent someone to see what the spiral could do...
So don't go to Rainbow Land,
Otherwise, you'll be sad.

Oliver Browne (8)
Ursuline Preparatory School, Warley

Football

Shoot, goal, whistle, kick,
Whee! I win!
Turn, skill, pass, *ouch*, fall...
Bang, scream, top bins, help!
Football is all of these things,
Just because I hit top bins.
I am the best football player,
No one can deny,
Since I won and the day is done.
For dessert, I get apple pie,
I look at the field and then I revealed,
I cheated at the game!
But please don't kick me out of the team,
This team is the best team I've ever dreamed.
So to make me feel better,
Can you buy me ice cream?
No! *You're out!*
Noooooo!
I am so sad.
Now that I am sad,
To make me feel glad,
Can you buy me ice cream?
No way!

Mia Holme (8)
Ursuline Preparatory School, Warley

The Time Travel

One hundred years, long ago,
Two girls were sleeping, as so.
These girls were special, as you know,
They went back one hundred years ago.

They saw them standing in a room,
The sky was sad and full of gloom.
We both heard footsteps and quickly ran,
Step, step, step, *creak*.

We quickly ran out the door
But I fell over, to the floor.
The woman chased us until we cried,
But we saw the woman, just right there
Chasing us, no time to spare!

We started spinning and bells were ringing,
But we woke up, back at the beginning!

Katerina Stowe-Mici (8)
Ursuline Preparatory School, Warley

Nature Bangs

Nature bangs,
Brown branches crack.

Owls howl and foxes sniff wolves up cliffs,
Snakes hiss and bite your wrist.

You may find out, it's a dangerous place,
And animals may eat your face.

Footprints, step by step,
From lots of bears.

Oh beware, oh beware,
You may be scared!
Don't ever go there,
It's a dangerous place.

And definitely - it is not safe!

Matilda Owolabi (7)
Ursuline Preparatory School, Warley

Magical Land

A small day in my life in Magical Land,
Pools, roller coasters and beaches with sand!
If you were to go here, have loads of fun,
You could be singing under the sun!

Popcorn and butterflies and coasters galore,
If you were to come here, you would want more!
The dancers and prancers and Rudolph Red Nose,
Santa and elves are sat on large shelves.

And Jingle Bells now ends with spells!

Nolah Mann (8)
Ursuline Preparatory School, Warley

Ranveer The Amazing Football Player

R onaldinho, his rainbow flicks are brilliant!
A ntonio is both a good scorer and a good defender
N eymar - his dribbling will make you dizzy
V an Dijk, you cannot get past him!
E rling Haaland has amazing skills, he will skill you up and make fun of you
E derson, his saves will make you annoyed
R onaldo - Siuuu! He is the world's top goalscorer.

Ranveer Sandhu (8)
Ursuline Preparatory School, Warley

The Upside Down Universe Of Dinos

On the ceiling - what is it?
It's a dino!
Why is it on the ceiling?
Because, well, I don't know.
Wait a sec - we're upside down!
I see dinosaurs...
T-rex, spinosaurus, paraceratherium,
Gigantopithecus, micropachycephalosaurus,
Basilosaurus, concavenator, plesiosaurus,
Mamenchisaurus, stegosaurus...
And my-tongue-is-tired-of-saying-o-saurus!

Henry Chase (7)
Ursuline Preparatory School, Warley

Iyla And Theodora's Friend'chip'

We were shaking hips while eating chips.
Then Theodora fell down a drain hole and nearly died.
A few minutes later, Iyla cried and made a pie.
An hour later, Iyla yelped whilst getting help.
Then a big grumpy man came to help Theodora out
And gave her a big dumpling.

Riddle:
What is easy to lose but hard to find?

Answer: A friend!

Iyla Dhillon (7)
Ursuline Preparatory School, Warley

Autumn

Leaves go red, orange and gold,
I crunch through the fallen leaves,
The smell of bonfires in the distance,
Smoke curls up into the sky.

My feet feel all crunchy from the leaves,
The special leaves are green and gold,
I feel so amazing in the wonderful weather,
I feel so free in this wonderful month!

Theadora Peers (8)
Ursuline Preparatory School, Warley

Diabolical Dinosaurs

D iabolical diabloceratops
I cy ichthyosaurus
N o more Mr Nice Guy
O bliterating baryonyx make you die!
S uper-duper supersaurus
A ggravated allosaurus
U nbelievable utahraptor, fear their vex!
R oaring rex!

Ryley Owen (11)
VLC, Leamington Spa

Dragons!

Dragons fly very high,
Up to the big, blue sky,
Dragons choking,
While they're smoking,
Out red-hot fire,
Dragons' caves are piled high,
With books and gold stacked up to the sky.

Rosie Benn (8)
Yarlside Academy, Barrow-In-Furness

YOUNG WRITERS INFORMATION

We hope you have enjoyed reading this book – and that you will continue to in the coming years.

If you're the parent or family member of an enthusiastic poet or story writer, do visit our website **www.youngwriters.co.uk/subscribe** and sign up to receive news, competitions, writing challenges and tips, activities and much, much more! There's lots to keep budding writers motivated!

If you would like to order further copies of this book, or any of our other titles, then please give us a call or order via your online account.

Young Writers
Remus House
Coltsfoot Drive
Peterborough
PE2 9BF
(01733) 890066
info@youngwriters.co.uk

Join in the conversation!
Tips, news, giveaways and much more!

YoungWritersUK YoungWritersCW

youngwriterscw youngwriterscw